Invasive
Freshwater Species

Linda M. Ivancic

Cavendish
Square

New York

Published in 2017 by Cavendish Square Publishing, LLC
243 5th Avenue, Suite 136, New York, NY 10016

Library of Congress Cataloging-in-Publication Data
Names: Ivancic, Linda.
Title: Invasive freshwater species / Linda M. Ivancic.
Description: New York : Cavendish Square Publishing, [2017] | Series: Invasive species | Includes index.
Identifiers: LCCN 2016005738 (print) | LCCN 2016010171 (ebook) |
ISBN 9781502618504 (library bound) | ISBN 9781502618511 (ebook)
Subjects: LCSH: Introduced freshwater organisms--Juvenile literature. |
Freshwater ecology--Juvenile literature.
Classification: LCC QH96.8.I57 I93 2017 (print) | LCC QH96.8.I57 (ebook) | DDC 333.95/23--dc23
LC record available at http://lccn.loc.gov/2016005738

Editorial Director: David McNamara
Editor: Renni Johnson
Copy Editor: Nathan Heidelberger
Art Director: Jeffrey Talbot
Designer: Alan Sliwinski
Production Assistant: Karol Szymczuk
Photo Research: J8 Media

The photographs in this book are used by permission and through the courtesy of: Vitalii Hulai/
Shutterstock.com, cover; Checubus/Shutterstock.com, 4; Steve Ruark/AP Images, 6; Sjgh/Shutterstock.
com, 8; Andrew Sacks/The LIFE Images Collection/Getty Images, 9 (left), Peter Yates/The LIFE Images
Collection/Getty Images, 9 (right); scubaluna/iStockphoto.com, 10; xjben/iStockphoto.com, 12; Carlyn
Iverson/Science Source/Getty Images, 14; Andy Bowlin/iStock/Thinkstock, 17; Jirateep Sankote/
Shutterstock.com, 18; Kittie and Minnie/Shutterstock.com, 20-21; Pete Saloutos/Getty Images, 22;
Gratefldiver Inc/Alamy Stock Photo, 24; Blickwinkel/Alamy Stock Photo, 26; Christopher David Howells/
Shutterstock.com, 27; M. Spencer Green/AP Images, 29; B toy Anucha/Shutterstock.com, 31; BSIP/
UIG/Getty Images, 32; Rick Bowmer/AP Images, 34; William Thomas Cain/Getty Images, 36; Education
Images/UIG/Getty Images, 38; Mcherevan/Shutterstock.com, 41.

Printed in the United States of America

CONTENTS

Invasive Freshwater Species

Freshwater habitats include lakes, ponds, streams, and rivers, and are found all over the world. Most freshwater habitats consist of moving water and contain many types of fish.

They Are Among Us

* * * * *

When you think of alien species, what comes to mind? How about an army of three-headed creatures slithering out of a UFO? The species this book will explore didn't travel across the universe to get here. These aliens are already among us, living in our lakes, rivers, and landscapes. Sometimes alien species are called exotic, **nonnative**, nonindigenous, or **invasive**. The term "invasive" is used for the most aggressive species, whose presence threatens habitats and native species.

Freshwater Invasive Species

Freshwater aquatic species are animals like fish and **mollusks** who call non-saltwater watery habitats home. These animals evolved in one location and were introduced into another. Once in a new home, the species is able to reproduce rapidly, become **established**, and often has negative impacts on the **aquatic ecosystem**.

Nonnative invaders can change how a habitat works by crowding out or taking the place of native species.

A "released" northern snakehead fish took over a freshwater habitat because it had no predators.

Such changes can even affect important human needs like the supply of water to our communities and whether food can be harvested from an area. They can also impact our experience of outdoor activities like hunting, fishing, camping, and boating.

Invasions by alien species are a worldwide occurrence. Invasive species make aquatic ecosystems some of the most threatened on the planet. It is not surprising that there are many fish species that are endangered in both freshwater and marine habitats.

Freshwater Takeover

Carried to North America from Europe in the **ballast** water of shipping vessels, zebra mussels were introduced when the ballast water was released into the Great Lakes. A zebra mussel is a mollusk that filters its food out of the water. The zebra mussels use the same food and space as native mussels. Female zebra mussels can produce up to one million eggs per year. Young zebra mussels attach themselves to hard surfaces. These surfaces include rocks, gravel, metal, crayfish, native mussels, and each other.

ZEBRA MUSSELS INVADE

Mississippi River

Hudson River

Lake St. Clair

Lake Mead

■ US States with Zebra Mussel Populations

Zebra mussels are tiny and reproduce in large numbers.

An inside view of a pipe filled with zebra mussels.

In 1988, Zebra mussels were first detected in Lake St. Clair, located between Lake Huron and Lake Erie. Within one year, they spread into all five of the Great Lakes.

In 1991, Zebra mussels spread into the rivers connected to the Mississippi River and also into the Hudson River.

In 2007, zebra and quagga mussels were discovered west of the Rocky Mountains for the first time, in Lake Mead, Nevada. They are now also found in Arizona, California, Colorado, Texas, and Utah.

Today, both species continue to spread into small lakes in the Great Lakes region and Maryland and Massachusetts where no populations had existed.

FRIEND OR FOE?

The round goby fish was accidentally introduced into the Great Lakes from the Black Sea via freighter ballast. The zebra mussel came a few years earlier and has a well-established invasive population throughout the Great Lakes. The goby loves to eat zebra mussels. Will the goby munch through the zebra mussel population to fuel a population surge of the round goby?

Round gobies love to snack on zebra mussels!

Big populations of mussels filter the water so well that they change the water in a harmful way for some sports fish. Thick colonies of zebra mussels can block water intake pipes for public water systems, industry, and power plants. They also spoil swimming areas with sharp shells.

Boating and fishing has unknowingly transferred zebra mussels from one body of water to another when they attach to hulls and travel in bait buckets. In a span of ten years, this tiny freshwater mussel has spread from one small lake to infest all five Great Lakes, most rivers in the Mississippi drainage basin, and Lake Mead in Nevada!

Fun activities like fishing or boating can disturb freshwater habitats if people aren't careful.

Welcome Mat

★ ★ ★ ★ ★

All species live in a place they call home. In the natural world, we call this home a habitat. The Earth has many habitats, such as oceans, forests, deserts, rivers, and lakes. Each habitat is unique, with differences in temperature, available food sources, and the amount of light and water that is present. A freshwater habitat also has a particular chemistry and flow to the water.

A habitat supplies the needs of the population that lives there. A natural home for a population of fish is a pond, river, or lake—a place full of water. Habitats can be as big as one of the Great Lakes or as small as a

An ecosystem consists of living things like the communities of plants and animals, as well as nonliving things like oxygen, water, soil, and rocks.

backyard koi pond. Many populations share a habitat. Fish live with mollusks, which also live with **plankton** in the water of the lake. Each habitat is a home to a complex community of **interdependent** organisms we call an **ecosystem**. Think of an animal's habitat like your home: your family is your population, your neighborhood is your community, and the city you live in is like an ecosystem.

A healthy ecosystem supports high **biological diversity**, or **biodiversity**. The variety of species and interacting relationships between all animals, plants, and their habitat creates a vibrant place to live. Invasive species are one of the greatest threats to biodiversity.

What Happens When a New Resident Moves In?

When a nonnative species moves into a habitat, it can cause dramatic changes. An invading species needs food, shelter, water, and a place to raise their young. If the invading species has the same needs as a native species, there is competition for the existing resources.

CLIMATE CHANGE

The Earth's climate is changing dramatically. Levels of atmospheric gases have caused changes in temperature and precipitation, which stresses ecosystems. Climate change affects how fish reproduce, grow, and where they can live. Habitats for fish that like cold waters, like salmon, may decrease, and habitats for fish who like warm water might expand. Recently, salmon have been migrating two weeks early to make certain they lay their eggs in cold water. Because salmon are a vital part of the food web, their schedule change will impact other fish and animals like birds, otters, and bears. As fish are confused by climate change, the whole ecosystem, and even our human use of fish, will need to adjust too.

Invading species can live alongside native species, but if the conditions are right, the invading species will overtake the native resident and even push natives out of their habitat.

This is what is happening to the common carp in the Mississippi River. When Asian carp were introduced, they quickly spread because they could out-compete the common carp and other native fish for food and space. The Asian carp's greedy eating habits are so successful at stripping native aquatic plants and mussels from the river that their presence actually caused the river water quality to change.

A habitat can become infested if it does not have the predators and conditions to stop an invader from taking over. What makes a habitat more likely to be invaded? Some habitats are vulnerable because of human activity as invading species may be more suited to the human-altered environment than the native animals.

Why Some Species Are Good Invaders

Some invaders have biological traits that make them more likely to survive over native species. Asian carp

The brown trout has few predators, including only bigger trout and humans, and has spread to every continent on Earth except Antarctica.

have a natural ability to out-compete native fish, including ciscos and yellow perch, for food. They also grow and reproduce more quickly. Some invaders can adapt to harsh or unusual conditions. For example, the northern snakehead fish can survive in a moist, out-of-water environment for up to three days and can even use its fins to push itself or "walk" short distances on land. The zebra mussel can survive out of the water for close to one month under the right conditions.

Why Some Habitats Get Invaded

Every species has a **niche** within a habitat. That describes the relationships and the role it has within a population. If a habitat has unused niches, an invading species might find a place or an opportunity to create a niche. Tilapia is a freshwater fish native to Africa. These fish require a warm-water home. They typically do not survive in **temperate** habitats. Tilapia is currently used in the Phoenix, Arizona, canal system

Habitats disturbed by people or natural disasters are at a greater risk of invasion.

to eat and help control algae growth. Yet, tilapia have spread to the colder waters of Idaho, where they do survive! They found a niche in the warm water that is released to rivers from power plants.

A disturbed ecosystem can contribute to the loss of native species. Humans cause disturbances like when a dam or fishing pier is built in a river. Other times, natural disruptions, such as floods, cause damage to freshwater ecosystems. Debris can alter the flow of moving water. If the food source for even one species is destroyed or reduced, the entire food chain will be disrupted. In a stressed or weakened habitat, native plants and fish struggle to thrive or support each other. A damaged ecosystem can offer a place for an invading species to set up a new home.

INVADERS THROUGHOUT THE WORLD

North America

Asian carp

Brown trout

Channeled apple snail

Common carp

Mosquito fish

Nile perch

Northern snakehead fish

Round goby

Sea lamprey

Tilapia

Zebra mussel

South America

Common carp

Mosquito fish

Tilapia

Europe

Common carp

Mosquito fish

Round goby

Sea lamprey

Zebra mussel

Africa

Common carp

Nile perch

Tilapia

Asia

Asian carp

Channeled apple snail

Common carp

ZEBRA MUSSEL

Europe

Asia

Africa

Australia

CHANNELED
APPLE SNAIL

Mosquito fish
Round goby
Snakehead fish
Tilapia
Zebra mussel

Australia
Channeled apple snail
Common carp
Mosquito fish

World travel, commerce, and international mail are among the many pathways that exotic species from all over the globe find their way to new places.

It's Our Home Too!

★ ★ ★ ★ ★

Plants and animals sometimes scatter naturally into new habitats when migrating for food or for spawning. Natural events like floods and storms also transport species to new locations. Most invasive species, however, are brought to new areas by people. Today, there is an ever-increasing and rapid movement of people and goods around the globe. Our transportation methods become pathways for invasive species. People in transit are the main **vectors** bringing invasive species to new areas—either accidentally or on purpose.

Accidental Stowaways

Zebra mussels arrived by hitching a ride in the ballast water of shipping vessels and were quick to roam to other nearby lakes. Movement of an invasive species from one habitat to another can happen naturally through a direct water connection like a river. It also happens when we move and carry infested water. Mussels are found in bait buckets; on boats, attached

Zebra mussels cause problems because they multiply quickly. Here they have taken over a sunken boat.

to hulls, motors, or trailers; and on other recreational equipment, like fishing and scuba gear.

Their spread has had an enormous impact on both the United States and Canada. Since their introduction thirty years ago, many hundreds of millions of dollars have been spent in the United States alone to control and get rid of this one invader species. From the tiny zebra mussel, we have learned that we need to pay close attention to the ways in which an invasive species can hitchhike around the world.

Invited Travelers

Invasive species can be introduced to a new location on purpose. Some people think that the new species will be useful to humans in its new location for various reasons.

The Nile perch is a species introduced as a new food source in Uganda's freshwater Lake Victoria. The goal was to increase the presence of a delicious food fish. Adding the Nile perch to the lake accomplished that goal, and a large fishing industry was created. However, the advancement of the Nile perch was at the expense of the lake's native species. The Nile

Fishing and releasing species into new habitats have unforeseen consequences.

perch fed upon the local fish, causing the extinction of several hundred different species. The choices we make in introducing can have unexpected short-term and long-term impacts.

Some people put new fish into lakes and rivers to help make the local fishing better. Fish have entered new waters by escaping from fish farms, and others have been "released" from their aquarium homes.

INTRODUCING THE GOLDFISH!

Goldfish and their relatives are now found in the wild in all fifty states.

Not all introduced species have negative effects. The common goldfish, a freshwater fish native to Asia, was one of the earliest fish to be domesticated and is one of the most commonly kept fish in an aquarium. Goldfish, along with other exotic fish, have been introduced to local waters when an aquarium is dumped. Now established or reported in all fifty states, there are many mutant goldfish varieties with a broad range of body forms and colors. The goldfish has not achieved "invasive" status and is not considered a "pest species," however, as its populations rarely get to large levels.

The northern snakehead fish is considered a valuable food fish and was brought to the United States for sale in pet stores and live food fish markets. The northern snakehead is an air-breathing freshwater fish that is native to Asia and Africa. In 2002, it was discovered that a released northern snakehead had expanded into a large population in a Maryland pond. This species was able to take over water habitats in the United States where it has no known predators. In only two years, the northern snakeheads had invaded and set up a permanent home in the Potomac River.

Some fish species have been introduced to control problems. Malaria is a mosquito-borne infectious disease of humans and other animals. Mosquito fish are freshwater fish that are named after one of the things they like to eat, namely mosquito larvae. Mosquito fish were intentionally introduced into habitats all over the world to control mosquitoes. In fact, they played a major role in wiping out malaria in South America, Russia, and Ukraine from the 1920s to the 1950s. In Sochi, Russia, there is even a monument to the mosquito fish in honor of its role in eliminating malaria.

Impacts on People

Invasive species cause a wide variety of problems, which almost always can be blamed on uncontrolled

Electric barriers are installed in rivers and channels to prevent fish, including invasive species, from spreading.

population growth and spread. There are economic impacts to businesses, food and sport fishing industries, and recreational areas. Many costs come from the efforts required to combat invasive species and reduce their rate of spread. In the United States, the expense is estimated to be more than $137 billion annually. We are also unaware of the potential health impacts that might occur to humans and wildlife as we use or dispose of the invasive species.

INVADERS TO NOTE

Channeled Apple Snail

Scientific name: *Pomacea canaliculata*

Description: Largest freshwater snail in North America, with a spherical shell height of 1.75 to 3 inches (45 to 75 millimeters). Color is brownish or greenish but can vary, with spiral, indented band patterns around the whorls. Opening is flared. Egg masses on plant or other structures above water surface are eye-catching pink.

Diet: Feeds voraciously on aquatic plants.

Predators: Insects, fish, amphibians, reptiles, crayfish, turtles, mammals, and birds.

Habitat: Lakes, ponds, canals, and swamps. Able to breathe in water and on land; can survive burrowed in mud for long periods of drought.

Place of Origin: South America, including Brazil, Bolivia, and Argentina.

Place of Relocation: Alabama, Florida, Texas, California, and Hawaii; also in Dominican Republic, Asia, Guam, Papua New Guinea, and Taiwan.

Cause of Introduction: Imported for use in the aquarium trade, as a food source, and for the biological control of weeds.

Did You Know: This snail is a serious wetland agricultural pest threatening the taro crop industry in Hawaii and rice production in Asia. The snail also serves as a vector for bacteria and parasites.

INVADERS TO NOTE

Common Carp

Scientific name: *Cyprinus carpio*

Description: Its body is large and thick with a length of 15 to 18 inches (38 to 46 cm), up to 47 inches (120 cm). It has noticeable barbels near corners of mouth. Its dorsal fin base is long with seventeen to twenty-one soft rays and a serrated trailing edge. Its scales are thick, large, and are usually olive grey on the back lightening to white or yellow on the belly.

Diet: Plants, animals, algae, fungi, and bacteria.

Predators: Other large fish like northern pike and largemouth bass; birds including herons, cormorants, goosanders; mammals including otters and minks.

Habitat: Streams, reservoirs, and lakes, in waters with high levels of organic matter.

Place of Origin: Asia and Europe

Place of Relocation: Most continents, fifty-nine countries

Year of Introduction in US: 1831

Cause of Introduction: Distributed all over the country by the government as a food fish.

Did You Know: The domesticated carp is highly tolerant of pollution and spreads through waters where most native species cannot live. In the early 1990s, biologists exposed control groups of carp to 1,600 chemicals commonly present in United States waters; only 135 of the pollutants killed all the fish.

Lamprey Eel

Scientific name: *Petromyzon marinus*

Description: Eel-like in appearance, but not an eel. The sea lamprey is a cartilaginous fish without jaws. This fish has two close dorsal fins, no paired fins, seven gill openings, and a sucking disc-shaped mouth funnel filled with hooked, sharp teeth radiating from the center.

Diet: Parasitic, feeding upon a wide range of fishes; the invasive populations played a major role in destroying native stocks of lake trout, whitefish, and walleye.

Predators: Humans

Habitat: Young sea lampreys are common in the silty bottoms of rivers and streams. Landlocked adult populations feed in open waters of large rivers and lakes.

Place of Origin: Generally marine, but moves to freshwater rivers to spawn. Along the Atlantic coast from Labrador to the Gulf of Mexico; landlocked in the Great Lakes and several New York lakes; Also the Atlantic coast of Europe and Mediterranean Sea.

Place of Relocation: Lake Ontario

Year of Introduction in US: 1835

Cause of Introduction: Access to Lake Ontario from rivers and streams that connect to the Erie Canal.

Did You Know: The Welland Canal opened in 1829 to bypass Niagara Falls and provide a route to Lake Erie from Lake Ontario. Almost a century passed before the fish were found in Lake Erie in 1921, yet within just twenty-five years, sea lampreys were in all the Great Lakes.

INVASIVE

Northern Snakehead

Scientific name:

Ophicephalus argus

Description:

Snakeheads have long, cylindrical bodies with a large mouth and sharp teeth. They have enlarged scales on top of their heads and their eyes are located far forward on their head, similar to the scale patterns and eye positions of snakes. Size and color patterns vary among twenty-nine recognized species. The largest recorded was 6 feet (1.8 meters) in length.

Diet: As young, they eat zooplankton, insect larvae, small crustaceans, and the young of other fish As adults, they feed on fish, crustaceans, frogs, small reptiles, and sometimes birds and small mammals.

Predators: Young are most at risk to other predatory fish (bass, perch, and pike) and wading birds. Adults are too large for most native fish. Humans are their greatest threat.

Habitat: Small and large streams, canals, rivers, ponds, reservoirs, and lakes.

Place of Origin: China, Russia, and Korea

Place of Relocation: Japan, Russia, Philippines, Madagascar, Hawaii, and mainland United States

Cause of Introduction: Imported for aquarium industry and food source.

Did You Know: Some young snakeheads are able to wriggle overland from one body of water to another, especially if the ground is wet. They flex their body, push with their tail, and use their broad pectoral fins to steady their head. It is unknown how far they can travel on land. The snakehead in Madagascar is known to crawl onshore, allow its body to be covered with ants, and return to the water where the ants are washed off and eaten by the fish!

Caution!

Don't Spread
New Zealand Mudsnails

Snails range in size from a grain of sand to 1/8 inch in length and are black or brown in color.

The Threat

◆ Rapid reproduction of this invader can lead to densities of 1 million per square yard. A single snail could result in the production of more than 40 million snails in one year.

◆ They outcompete and replace native invertebrates that are the preferred foods of fish.

◆ They can cause drastic, harmful changes in the native plant and animal food web of streams and lakes.

What You Can Do

◆ If you wade, freeze waders and other gear overnight (at least 6 hours).

◆ Have extra waders and boots that are used only in infested waters. Store them separately.

◆ After leaving the water, inspect waders, boots, float tubes, boats/trailers-any gear used in the water. Remove visible snails with a stiff brush and follow with rinsing. If possible, freeze or completely dry out any wet gear.

◆ Never transport live fish or other aquatic animals or plants from one water to another.

CALIFORNIA TROUT

www.caltrout.org

FEDERATION OF FLY FISHERS

TROUT UNLIMITED

This sign warns boaters to be cautious about spreading invasive mudsnails. Education and awareness are important to control invasive species.

No
Vacancy

★ ★ ★ ★ ★

Is there anything that can be done to prevent invasive species from moving in? What can we do to get rid of the invasive populations? Keeping invaders out is the best way to prevent nonnative species from becoming a problem. We do that by watching the pathways that invaders use to get here—such as in ballast water and releasing fish into local waters.

Four methods have been used to control aquatic invasive species: physical removal, ecological, chemical, and biological control.

Physical removal is best when the invasion just starts, when the population is small and contained to a specific area. In a water habitat, this may mean using nets and physical methods to remove the fish, mollusks, or infested water.

Ecological control alters the ecosystem in some way, like changing the water levels or water flow, to disturb the life cycle of the invader. If done carefully, it will not hurt native species and will give them an advantage to help them compete with the invasive species.

Chemical control uses chemical pesticides to kill invaders. While chemical control is widely used against invasive species on land, it is rarely an option in open water systems. Chemicals are hard to control and may get into drinking water.

Biological control involves introducing an enemy of an invasive species, such as a disease, parasite, predator, or **competitor**, to try to control the invader. This may result in the enemy becoming a new invasive species population!

Help Stop the Spread

Here are some things you can do to help prevent the introduction and spread of aquatic invasive species:

FIGHTING INVASIVE SPECIES, ONE BITE AT A TIME!

Invasivorism explores the idea of eating invasive species in order to control, reduce, or eliminate their populations. The animal must be a problem because of its overabundance, such as the Asian carp that have been dominating the Mississippi River over the last several years. In a similar way, Target Hunger Now! in Illinois is encouraging anglers to donate Asian carp for processing into healthy, ready-to-serve meals. This effort is designed to feed communities while reducing the Asian carp threat. Worldwide, chefs have begun seeking out and using invasive species as alternative ingredients in new recipes. Grilled Asian carp tacos, anyone?

Next time you eat out, check the menu specials for invasive species, such as the lamprey eel.

- Learn to recognize common invaders.
- Inspect, drain, and clean boats, kayaks, and other recreational gear after use.
- Buy pets from reputable dealers whose nonnative animals are properly labeled, legally imported, and not harboring invasive pests and diseases.
- Do not release live fish, bait, or aquarium fish (or water) into local waters.
- Join a volunteer group that works to control invasive species. Contact your state or county invasive species committee or local nonprofit organizations, such as the Sierra Club.

Human activity has caused the worldwide invasion of nonnative species. It is our challenge to come up with solutions to this complex concern. There is no one-size-fits-all solution. As each species causes unique problems to the environment, solving the problems and getting rid of or limiting the spread must be handled differently each time. We can protect freshwater ecosystems when countries around the world work together to prevent the spread of invasive species.

GLOSSARY

aquatic ecosystem An ecosystem in a body of water; communities of organisms that are dependent on each other and on their environment.

ballast Heavy material such as rocks or water that is put on a ship to make it steady.

biological diversity or **biodiversity** The amount of variety in the different plants, animals, and other species in a given habitat at a particular time; a measure of how healthy an ecosystem is.

competitor A species that shares the same environment and competes for resources such as water, food, and shelter.

ecosystem All the living and nonliving things in an area; a variety of populations living in community and interacting with the nonliving portions of the area.

establish The process by which a nonnative species in a new habitat successfully produces offspring with the chance of survival.

interdependent People, animals, or things depending on each another.

invasive species A nonnative species whose introduction and spread outside their natural range harms or threatens biological diversity, economies, or human health.

mollusk Any of a large family (Mollusca) of invertebrate animals (as snails, clams, or squids) with a soft unsegmented body usually enclosed in a shell and living in both freshwater and salt water.

niche The role and position of an organism or population within a community.

nonnative species A species introduced outside its natural past or present range; including the members that survive and reproduce.

plankton The collection of mostly small or microscopic organisms that drift or swim in a body of water.

temperate Characterized by moderate temperatures, weather, or climate; neither hot nor cold.

vector Any living or nonliving thing that transports living organisms, either deliberately or accidentally.

FIND OUT MORE

Books

Barrett-O'Leary, Marilyn. *Oh No! Hannah's Swamp is Changing*. Baton Rouge, LA: Louisiana Sea Grant College Program, Louisiana State University, 2002.

Collard, Sneed B. *Science Warriors: The Battle Against Invasive Species*. Scientists in the Field. Boston, MA: HMH Books for Young Readers, 2008.

Latta, Sara L. *Keep Out!: Invasive Species*. Nature's Invaders. North Mankato, MN: Capstone Press, 2013.

Websites

Aquatic Nuisance Species (ANS) Task Force
www.anstaskforce.gov/default.php
The Aquatic Nuisance Species (ANS) Task Force consists of thirteen federal agencies and other private interests dedicated to preventing and controlling aquatic nuisance species. The site includes good fact sheets on "Species of Concern."

Defending Favorite Places: How Hunters and Anglers Can Stop the Spread of Invasive Species

www.fs.fed.us/invasivespecies/prevention/defending.shtml

The documentary video was produced as part of the National Invasive Species Threat Campaign and links the management of invasive species with hunting and angling conservation.

Habitattitude

www.habitattitude.net

This site is for aquarium hobbyists, backyard pond owners, water gardeners, and others who are concerned with protecting aquatic resources.

National Invasive Species Information Center (NISIC)

www.invasivespeciesinfo.gov/aquatics

Gateway to invasive species information; covers federal, state, local, and international sources.

US Geologic Survey NAS - Nonindigenous Aquatic Species

nas.er.usgs.gov

Information resource pages include updated distribution maps identifying locations and spread of aquatic invasive species by region.

INDEX

Page numbers in **boldface** are illustrations. Entries in **boldface** are glossary terms.

ABOUT THE AUTHOR

Linda Ivancic comes to writing children's science books after twenty-eight years as an environmental, health and safety consultant. Linda's desire to explore the natural world started at her family home along the shore of Lake Ontario. Each day the lake invited closer investigation of nature at work in the waves, fish, and sea birds within this freshwater ecosystem. Linda Ivancic has published other science books with Cavendish Square for middle school students, including *What Is a Wave?*, *What Is the Color Spectrum?*, and *What Is Wind?* A sympathetic Pisces, she has liberated many "fisherman's catch-of-the-day" back to the wild. Linda lives in western New York—adjacent to the freshwater treasures of Lake Erie, the Niagara River, and Lake Ontario—with her husband and their 75-gallon aquarium of freshwater fish.